THE
SCORING
ZONE

How to hit the shots that matter, when you need them most.

TODD
SONES

with Matthew Rudy

Printed in the United States of America

First Printing, 2018

ISBN-13: 978-0692128893
ISBN-10: 0692128891

Todd Sones
Impact Golf/Scoring Zone Schools
White Deer Run Golf Club
250 West Greggs Pkwy
Vernon Hills, IL 60061
toddsones.com

Cover design: Chris David (edoagency.com)
Interior design: Tim Oliver (timothypoliver.com)
All photography provided by Hector Padilla
(hpadillaprgolf@yahoo.com)

To my dad, Charlie, and my sons, CJ and Owen, whom I love dearly. My dad inspired me to take up the game so I could spend more time with him. CJ and Owen always inspire me to be an example to them as a better person who helps others and does the best he can with what he is given.

CONTENTS

"The shots you'll learn in this book will get you asking better questions around the green, and feeling more confident that you have the best answers. *The Scoring Zone* will help you reduce your unforced short game errors, and have more fun when you play. I'm excited for you to read it."
— STAN UTLEY, *Golf Digest 50 Best Teacher and PGA Tour winner*

"Todd's book is filled with terrific short game information, but it is much more than that. He gives you an organized way to incorporate the information into your game to really improve your score. I recommend him—and his book—to anybody who wants to play better golf from 100 yards in."
— MARTIN CHUCK, *Golf Magazine Top 100 Teacher*

"In *The Scoring Zone*, you'll find the key elements to building a short game that will be the envy of your playing partners. I've been fortunate to have Todd's help during my career, and his reputation as a top teacher speaks for itself. Use the fundamentals in this book and I promise you'll see that scoring average come down. I know mine has."
— JOE DURANT, *PGA Tour winner*

"I've known Todd for more than 20 years, and he's a professional through and through. His excellent teaching skills have made the difference for everyone from PGA Tour players to high-handicappers. It's very refreshing to know a person who cares so deeply for helping players get better."
— STEVE JONES, *1996 U.S. Open champion*

YEARS AGO, when I was first moving from playing to coaching, I came to Chicago to give a short game presentation for the Illinois PGA section at their instruction summit. I like to present outside and hit real shots, so I was on a green with a big group of teachers surrounding me. I decided to pick somebody at random to come out and roll some putts so I could explain my approach and offer some advice.

Todd was my random "test subject," and at the time I didn't know about his record as a terrific short game instructor. He made a lot of putts that day without my help (and put up with some good-natured teasing about his stroke), and we started what has become a terrific friendship. I always enjoy my time with Todd because we have a lot in common— from our Christian faith to our commitment to helping players enjoy the short game more. Todd's teaching philosophy is also right in line with mine, in that he's constantly influenced by the time he spends with other teachers and his students. He's always learning.

The result of all that learning is pulled together for you here, in *The Scoring Zone*. I like to tell my students that the best questions win— because they inspire the most important answers. Todd's proven techniques do exactly that. The shots you'll learn in this book will get you asking better questions around the green, and feeling more confident that you have the best answers. You'll be excited to go out and work on your short game, because you'll have the right plan in place to see real improvement and avoid the frustration that sends a lot of players directly to the range to bash drivers with all their practice time.

The Scoring Zone will help you reduce your unforced short game errors, and have more fun when you play. I'm excited for you to read it.

STAN UTLEY

Golf Digest 50 Best Teacher

PGA Tour winner

Grayhawk Golf Club, Scottsdale

WHEN I WAS STARTING OUT as an instructor a couple of decades ago, I did what a lot of motivated young teachers do. I traveled around looking for the best information I could find to improve my teaching. I'd ask experienced teachers if I could observe them teach a few lessons, and I went to every teaching seminar that seemed to have even a hint of value.

Luckily, Todd Sones was giving one of those seminars. Even though Todd was a young guy at the time, he had already accomplished a lot. I was immediately impressed by his presentation—both because of his material and how he communicated it. He cared about connecting with the people in the audience, and his passion for the subject was so obvious.

Todd was an inspiration. He showed me that a young guy could find success in this business. He also proved that you don't have to be afraid to specialize. Todd is a terrific full swing teacher, but he really makes an impression in the scoring zone, teaching players how to improve their short game shots.

Over the years, Todd has been so generous with other teachers—helping them improve their own technique and how they share short game instruction. Those teachers have then been able to take that information and spread it to their own students.

Todd's book is filled with terrific short game information, but it is much more than that. He gives you an organized way to incorporate the information into your game to really improve your score. I recommend him—and this book—to anybody who wants to play better golf from 100 yards in.

MARTIN CHUCK
Golf Magazine Top 100 Teacher
Tour Striker Golf Schools
Phoenix, AZ

FOR THE FIRST 15 YEARS OF MY TEACHING CAREER, I spent my time doing what the members at my clubs asked me to do. They'd come into the shop looking for a lesson on improving their full swing, and I'd give them those lessons. In that era, before most people had ever heard of specialized short game instruction, nobody ever came in and asked specifically for help with their putting or wedges.

The truth is, I never got any of those students to their peak scoring potential, because they didn't ask for that kind of help—and we didn't spend much time working on those parts of their games.

It wasn't until I started my Todd Sones Impact Golf School in 1997 that I began to see the instruction gap most players were falling into. They were leaving so many shots on their scorecards because they couldn't "finish"—or get the ball into the hole efficiently from 100 yards and in.

That "Scoring Zone" has become the emphasis of my teaching in the last two decades, and it has transformed the thousands of students who have come through my program at White Deer Run Golf Club in Vernon Hills, IL, outside Chicago.

Transformation can sound like an exaggeration, but let me tell you why it isn't in this case.

Whether you're a PGA Tour player or a 20-plus handicapper, a third of your score is determined from the edge of the green out to the distance that constitutes less than a full shot with your sand wedge. A tour player can hit a sand wedge 115 or 120 yards. Thirty percent of his score is determined by the shots he hits from about 100 yards in to the edge of the green. For the average handicap player who comes to see me for one of my schools, that span is from about 85 yards to the edge of the green.

That's the Scoring Zone—and it's where you dramatically improve your handicap without tearing your swing down and starting from scratch. You can *transform* your scorecard over the course of a school—or by reading a book.

On these pages, I'm going to show you the same techniques, tips and strategies that I share in my Scoring Zone schools every summer. They're the same techniques that my 100-shooting students have incorporated on their way to breaking 80, and the same ones I've used with tour students like Scott McCarron, Robert Gamez, Shaun Micheel, Jay Williamson, Steve Jones, Paul Goydos, Joe Durant, Stephanie Loudon and Hilary Lunke.

You'll understand not only how to hit the shots you need from the hundred-yard plate and in, but when to hit them.

We'll break the Scoring Zone down into its component parts. You'll learn to improve what I call your "mini-wedge" game—the off-speed wedge shots tour players are so good at judging, from 100 yards down to about 20 yards off the green. You'll dial in your pitching game from 20 yards and in, and learn what I call the "Pinch shot" and the "High Slider". We'll finish with the versatile explosion shot that will make you much more reliable out of the rough and the sand.

Once you understand this relatively simple menu of techniques, you'll be able to pick the right one for the scenario you face and commit to your shot choice with confidence. When you have the technique and the confidence, you have command of your short game.

You're ready to score—and to find out what your scoring potential really is!

TODD SONES
Golf Magazine Top 100 Teacher
Golf Digest 50 Best Teacher
Two-Time Illinois PGA Teacher of the Year
Three-Time Illinois Horton Smith Award

CHAPTER 1

SCORING GAME PRINCIPLES

WHAT IS THE GOAL with any short game shot?

It is to put you in a better position to score. That can mean going from a perfect lie 50 yards out in the middle of the fairway to a makeable putt, or it can mean just escaping a brutal lie in the deep grass next to the green and getting into position to two-putt.

Both scenarios—and all the ones in between—rely on a basic set of techniques that allow you hit the right kind of shot at the right time. They let you hit the shot with the highest probability of a good outcome.

But for a lot of players, that "good outcome" doesn't come from a specific plan, or from a particular kind of technique. A lot of players don't pick a specific shot to hit, visualize what that shot will do and then execute the shot.

They play without a plan, and without a specific idea of *how* to hit a shot that matches the situation. Without those elements, there's no way to develop any confidence in your short game. You're hitting and hoping. Hope is not a good plan (or a good swing thought). You're also putting a lot of pressure on the other parts of your game. When you don't feel good about your pitching or sand game, for example, you're going to spend a lot of time trying to avoid situations where you have to hit those shots. You'll be playing a lot of defensive golf, and adding a ton of stress. You're playing with fear instead of confidence.

We're about to change that.

Starting with the baseline fundamentals in this chapter, you'll be able to spend just a fraction of the time it would take to dramatically change your full swing, but make improvements that have a huge impact on your overall scoring. For the average 80- or 90-something shooter , an investment of 10 or 15 percent more short game practice time will produce 40 or 50 percent of the scoring improvement.

There's no better way to spend your practice time.

Let's talk about what you can get out of it.

You'll be learning about a variety of different short game shots with interesting names that make them easier to remember—like the low trap, the high slider and the bunker explosion—but even before we get to the particular details of those, let's break things down to a more fundamental level.

On *every* short game shot, you need a plan, and you need a process that will let you hit the shot *intentionally*. What does "intentionally" mean? That you're making the kind of contact you want to make on purpose.

For a basic chip or pitch from a good lie, that means making solid contact and getting the ball to go where you expect it to go. From the bunker, it means making the club interact with the sand the way you expect. From a terrible lie in the rough, it means creating the best chance for the club to get through the grass and pop the ball out with some semblance of control over how far it flies and rolls.

Does it mean every shot will always come off exactly right? Of course not. Even tour players don't hit perfect short game shots every time. But if you have a plan and a comfortable familiarity with what you need to do for a particular shot, you start playing with confidence.

The game gets more fun. You'll be excited to play your next round, and you'll look forward to the chance to test your short game skills.

THE FUNDAMENTALS

You've probably read and watched a lot of short game lessons in maga-zines or on videos, and you've probably seen tons of different descriptions about how to hit a variety of shots. Watch enough of that stuff and you'll come away with the thought that there can't really be "fundamentals" in short game because there are so many different ways people describe how to hit these shots!

Open stance. Closed stance. Ball up. Ball back. Body turn. Body quiet.

It can certainly be confusing, and it isn't surprising that a lot of play-ers get out to the course and either fall back to the technique they've al-ways used or make a swing that's a messy combination of a lot of different half-digested tips.

My goal in The Scoring Zone is to show that there really are fundamen-tals that apply to virtually every short game shot, and when you under-stand those fundamentals, you have a base from which you can deal with any scenario.

When you see the logic behind the fundamentals, you can make adjust-ments to your setup and your swing that support what you're trying to do.

Let me show you how.

The very first fundamental I teach at the beginning of any Scoring Zone school or initial lesson is that the clubhead always **descends** through im-pact on a good short game shot. One analogy I like to use with my stu-dents is a plane moving through the air. When you make a swing with a descending clubhead path through impact, you're essentially landing the plane. When you're hitting up on the shot, the plane is leaving the runway. When you make an ascending swing on any shot besides one when the ball is on a tee, you're running the risk of skulling or chunking it (*right*).

To me, making the club descend through impact—making it land, so to speak—is the foundation of a good short game, so we'll start there. When players struggle with this fundamental, it's usually because they're making

When the clubhead descends through impact (*above*), the ball flies into the air, as compared to the ascending skulled and chunked shots below.

NO

This bad setup position is really common. The ball is too far back, the shoulders are dramatically tilted, and the club is angled toward the target and forward of the chest.

a setup mistake or because they're making the incorrect swing motion.

Let's use a basic chip shot as an example. Many, many players have heard that you should play the ball back in your stance for this shot, turn your feet toward the target in an open stance, push the handle forward (which tilts the upper body too far back) and then try to hit down on the ball.

But when you push the handle forward past the center point of your body—the center of your sternum—you're forced into a position where your trailing shoulder is too low and your lead shoulder is too high (*left*). Your spine is tilted back, away from the target, which makes it very hard to create that descending swing. You've basically preset yourself to swing up. The other big mistake that creates an upward blow comes in how the swing itself is sequenced. When you hit a shot, you're using 3 major moving parts. Your lower body, upper body and arms all obviously move, as does the club. The sequencing you need depends on the kind of shot you're hitting. When you make a full swing with, say, a fairway wood, you use a ground-up sequence. Your lower body initiates the downswing, followed by the upper body and then the arms and lastly the club. As the lower body slows down through impact, the energy generated there transfers to the upper body, and so on. That sequence is designed to produce maximum clubhead speed—to hit the ball the full distance for the club you're using.

But on this little chip shot we're describing, you don't need maximum clubhead speed. When you use that same kind of sequencing—starting with the lower body—on what I call a "finesse" shot, you have way too much energy or speed for the shot you need. Your mind knows this, and puts on the brakes hard down by the ball. Your upper body pulls back to decelerate the clubhead, and that move pulls the clubhead upward. (*next page*). Result, skull or chunk!

To consistently get the clubhead descending through your short game shots, you need to follow four basic principles to get that plane landing,

When the legs drive, the upper body
hangs back and the clubhead lags.

When you hang back with the upper body the hands
tend to flip as the club bottoms to early.

not taking off. These four principles—which we're going to go through below—are ones you can use for virtually *any* short game shot, from the shortest, lowest chip to the highest flop. Get good at these four things and you'll have the blueprint for a strong short game.

1. STAND TO THE HANDLE with a neutral spine.

"Stand to the handle" seems like simple advice—after all, the club is right there in front of you, isn't it? IT IS. You can actually use the club to guide you into an ideal setup position—one that gets the club in right position to make good contact with the ball and the ground while also keeping your spine in a neutral position.

To stand to the handle, start by finding what I call your natural grip. With the club soled flat on the ground, set your left (or lead) hand grip while your arm is hanging straight down naturally, hand beside your hip— not by extending your arms out in front of you like most players do (*right*). The club should be in your fingers—not across your palm—and you should be able to hinge the club upward at the wrist joint with virtually no effort.

Once you have your left hand set, bring your right (or trail) across and put that into place so that the lifeline on your right palm is running down the top of your left thumb. With your grip centered in front of you, you should be able to look down and see the Vs created by your thumbs and index fingers pointing at your right shoulder.

By setting your grip this way, you're preserving the natural up-and-down lever in your wrists, so that they work the way they should on the various short game shots we're going to talk about. If you set your grip with your arms extended and the club out in front of you, it's more likely that you'll establish a grip that blocks off your wrist hinge, or that sets your hands and club at an unnatural angle that will force you to make an adjustment to your body when you get in your stance.

With this natural grip, the butt of the club should be pointing up right

YES LEAD ARM HANGING, GRIP IN FINGERS

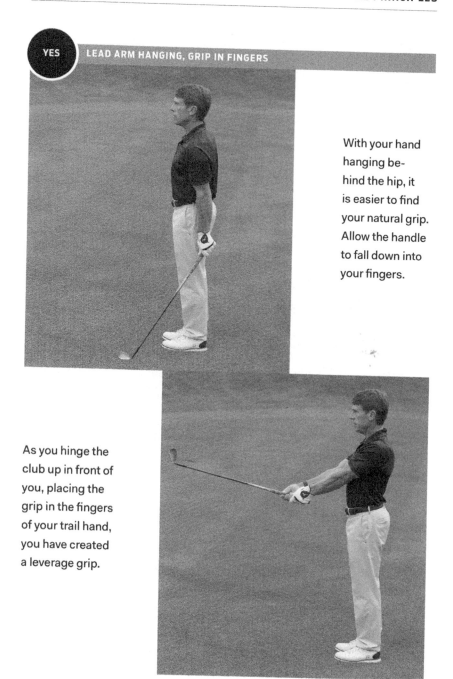

With your hand hanging behind the hip, it is easier to find your natural grip. Allow the handle to fall down into your fingers.

As you hinge the club up in front of you, placing the grip in the fingers of your trail hand, you have created a leverage grip.

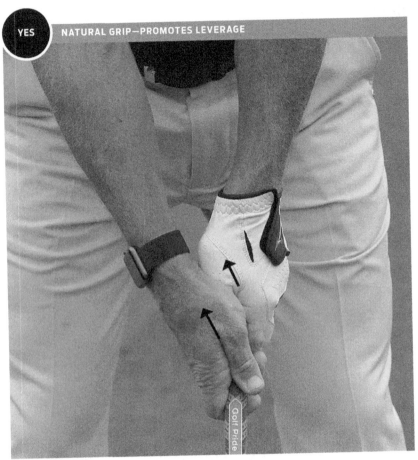

YES | **NATURAL GRIP—PROMOTES LEVERAGE**

When the handle of the club is sitting deeper in the fingers, it is like squeezing water out of a wash cloth. The hands rotate toward each other.

between your arms into the middle of your chest—just barely forward of the buttons on your shirt—when the club is soled on the ground (*above*). From a neutral, center ball position, the club will then be the guide you need to set the face aimed at your target, your feet set in relation to the clubhead, your shoulders level and your chest and spine neutral and in line with what you've established with the club. The beauty of this process

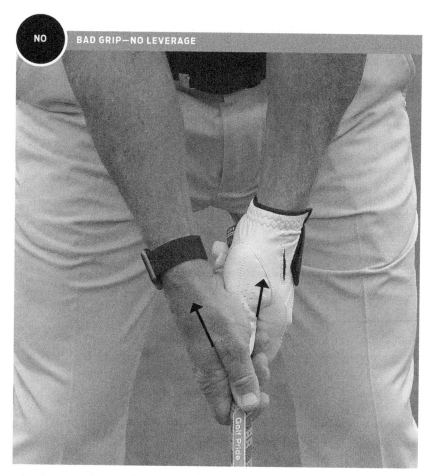

NO   BAD GRIP—NO LEVERAGE

Check out the arrows created by my thumbs and the sides of my hands. They're pointed opposite of each other, instead of both aimed at my right shoulder as they should be.

is that when you need to make adjustments to play a different kind of shot, the handle will still be your guide.

A "neutral spine" means you're in a comfortable, balanced setup with your spine perpendicular to the ground. If you try to play short game shots (or any shots, really) with your spine tilted dramatically forward or backward, you're forcing yourself to make compensations with your hands and arms to account for the bad body position. As we talked about earlier, pushing the shaft forward to hit a chip shot creates a scenario where the spine is tilted back, away from the ball. That setup promotes a swing that bottoms out too early. When you play short game shots, you want the handle centered with *your* center—so that if you pulled the grip toward you, it would hit your belt buckle (*right*).

2. Initiate the downswing with the clubhead

Short game shots are about precision and finesse, not speed. Instead of multiplying your swing speed with a lower-body-initiated downswing in the power sequence we described earlier, you want to start things off with your clubhead on these short shots. Instead of producing a swing where the clubhead lags behind, you're making one where you *throw* the clubhead right away, so it doesn't lag. In fact, lag is one of the two "L's" I call short game destroyers. The other is "lateral," which we'll be talking about later.

If you picture your swing from face-on, imagine your clubhead, hands and chest all making their own circles during the swing. The clubhead makes the largest circle, followed by the hands and the center of the body—which is making the smallest circle of the three. The goal is to get the clubhead, hands and body center to reach the impact point of their circles all at the same time.

For this to happen, the clubhead has farther to go, which means it needs to start earlier and move faster. That means you're going to feel a different sensation from the top of the backswing than you're probably used to with your full swing. Instead of starting your downswing with a lower body drive while your hands swing down toward the ball, your first move in the downswing will be releasing the clubhead and making it start its trip toward the ball (*next page*). I like to use the analogy of a horse race going around a circular track. The horse in the outside lane is the clubhead, and it needs to go the fastest to get around the track first.

YES STAND TO THE HANDLE—NEUTRAL SPINE

In a great setup, your shoulders are more level, and the shaft is aimed right at the center of your body. Compare this to the bad position in page 6.

YES CLUBHEAD LEADS, BODY FOLLOWS

1.

On all shots
start by,
STANDING TO
THE HANDLE.

2.

When the
clubhead
leads the tran-
sition...

...the club-head, hands and body center align perfectly at impact.

Your upper body transfers your weight to your forward leg.

DRILL — PROPER DOWNSWING SEQUENCE — THROW THE BALL

A great way to feel this new sensation is to get in your golf posture and address a ball on the ground normally, but hold a ball in your right hand instead of a club. Go to the top of your backswing and throw that ball down at the ball on the ground. If you're producing "lag," you won't be able to hit the target ball on the ground (*above*).

3. Stable lower body and pivot on top of the lead hip.

This element goes hand in hand (so to speak) with the previous one. Short game shots are upper-body-dominated shots, initiated from the top of the downswing by moving the clubhead *first*. Students often ask me what the lower body is supposed to do during the swing, and my answer is simple: Respond. You don't want to be actively shifting your lower body back or

To feel a good downswing sequence, hold a ball in your right hand, go to the top of the backswing and throw the ball down to a ball on the ground.

through. You want to stay stable, but let your legs respond to what your upper body is doing.

When you need to turn your chest back, your hips and thighs won't be frozen. They'll move slightly to accommodate the movement of your upper chest. And when you swing down through the ball, you want to feel like you're pivoting around a post stuck in the ground and coming up through the top of your lead hip.

It's easy to see when this goes wrong. If your tendency is to make an aggressive shift with your lower body toward the target, this will force your upper body to fall back—and the club will bottom out too early. This is the other "L" death move, "lateral," I mentioned before.

To feel the correct movement, I like to ask students to picture turning

and handing a heavy sandbag to somebody in front of them (*above*), or turning to dump a bucket of water on the ground in front of the ball. Both of those moves require the lower body to provide support and stability—not be super active and moving around.

4. Grip pressure increases through impact.

The last principle touches on something you've probably heard talked about before: Grip pressure. You've probably heard teachers or players talk about keeping a light grip pressure for feel, or keeping a constant grip pressure throughout the swing.

I prefer a different principle, because I think it helps promote the right movements from your arms and wrists through the downswing. It also

To feel less lateral movement in your short swings,
hold a heavy sandbag and
turn to toss it toward the
target. You need lower
body stability to do it.

helps make sure the clubhead is stable and square through impact. Take
your normal grip and hold the club in a light-but-controlled tension level,
but as you make your short game swing down through impact, *increase*
your grip pressure.

Most players tend to hold onto the club too tightly at address all the
way up to transition, which usually forces them to let go as they strike the
ball, losing control of the clubhead. If you measured your grip tension on
a scale from 1 to 10, with 1 being the club almost falling out of your hands
and 10 being the club getting crushed in a vice, I'd suggest using 3 tension
at address through transition, increasing to 6 or 7 at impact.

This goes against what you might have heard or read about in short
game instruction over the years. But after years of teaching and examining

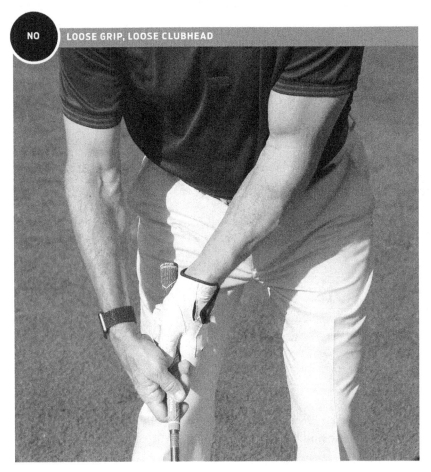

NO   LOOSE GRIP, LOOSE CLUBHEAD

If you hold the grip too loosely, you' ll loose control of the clubhead at impact.

my own short game technique, I've come to understand how important this concept is.

A visit from one of my low single-digit handicap players a few years ago is a perfect example of what I'm describing. My student flew in from the East Coast because he had been having a terrible time with what he described as a case of the chipping yips.

We started the lesson working on the exact fundamentals I've been de-

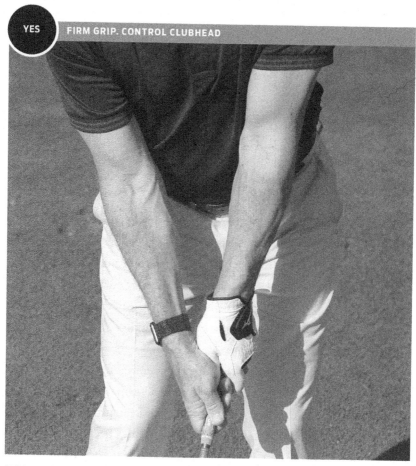

YES FIRM GRIP. CONTROL CLUBHEAD

With a grip that is firmer through impact, you can deliver
the clubhead precisely to the ball.

scribing in this chapter. Even after improving his setup position and sequencing, he still seemed to yip at impact. I decided to take some closeup
video of his hands through impact to see what was going on. When I did,
you could see that the handle of the club was literally coming out of his
hands at impact. He clearly didn't have control over the clubface as he was
contacting the ball.

I asked what he was working on in terms of tension in his hands. He said he was trying to use constant, light grip pressure, as if he was holding a live bird—Sam Snead's classic tip. It's something I had certainly told students earlier in my career.

But the reality of clubface control is more toward a tight grip than a loose, uncontrolled one. I asked my student to firm up his grip pressure through impact, so that he was squeezing at a 7 when the clubhead got to the ball. In a matter of one ball, the yips were gone.

He just needed to feel that control.

The amount you need to increase pressure depends on the kind of shot you have in front of you (*previous page*). For all shots, you'd start with about a 3 on that 1-10 scale. On a putt, you might only increase to a 4. For a driver, you'd increase to an 8. For short game shots, you'd want to increase more for shots that provide more resistance because of the lie. That means a 6 or 7 for a shot from deep grass or from the sand.

Go to a short game practice area and experiment for yourself to find the variables that work the best for you. But the overarching point is that you want to forget about the idea of a consistent, soft grip pressure.

It might sound like an oversimplification, but I can promise you it isn't. Every miss you experience in the scoring zone comes because of a breakdown in one of these four fundamentals. When you have command of them, you're well on your way to building the confidence all great short game players have.

Let's take a look at how to do that in greater detail, for each Scoring Zone shot.

KEY POINTS—

Most Important Fundamental:

The clubhead must DESCEND through the ball

Four principles for the clubhead to DESCEND:

1. Stand to the Handle
2. Initiate downswing with the clubhead
3. Upper body transfers weight over lead leg
4. Firmer grip pressure at impact than at address

NOTES

CHAPTER 2

THE
MINI-WEDGE

WHEN PLAYERS THINK ABOUT working on the "short game," they tend to do a few stereotypical things. They'll go to the practice green with a sleeve of balls and mess around for 20 minutes hitting some short green-side shots without much of a purpose. Or, if they're fortunate enough to have access to a facility like we have here at White Deer Run, they go to a dedicated short game area and get a small bucket of balls and hit a whole bunch of the same shot, over and over again.

I'm not suggesting that either of those activities are a waste of time. If you're paying attention to the feedback you get on those shots, you can get some value there.

But if you're truly interested in improving your total scoring game, you have to understand what shots go into scoring—and put in productive, efficient work on each kind of shot.

"Short game" usually gets categorized as chip and pitch shots hit from near the green—and those are important to know how to do. But this leaves out an extremely important part of the short game that is crucial to any player interested in scoring. In fact, it's an area of the game that's *more* important for players at higher handicaps.

I call it the mini-wedge, and there's a reason we're going to cover it first—before chips and pitches.

The mini-wedge is any shot you'd hit from less-than-full wedge distance down to about 20 yards off the green. The mini-wedge works as a kind of transition from your full swing toward the more specialized swings you're going to make when you get close to the green. Your stance and setup is similar to what you'd use for a full short iron shot, but your focus is much more on control and consistency than speed.

Getting good at mini-wedge shots is extremely valuable, because improving your sequence of motion and quality of strike on these shots not only makes you more precise and helps save you shots in the short term, but also improves the quality of your full swing.

You're getting two kinds of improvement at once.

And since mini-wedge shots often present themselves in strategically important situations—say, when you've hit a bad tee shot and couldn't get to the green for your approach shot, or when you've hit two great shots on a par-5 and have a chance to set up an easy birdie try (or lock down a par), they're a huge part of your scoring game.

THE PROBLEM

A nice, full swing with a pitching wedge or a 9-iron is a shot most players feel pretty good about, even at higher handicap levels. But when that shot changes to, say, a 50-yarder, the reduction in distance just seems to crank up the anxiety and difficulty levels.

Why?

After all, shouldn't a shorter shot that doesn't require as much speed or strength be an easier one to hit?

Not the way most players play it.

Most players struggle with mini-wedges from less-than-full distances because they make two key mistakes. They take the club back way too far, and they do it from a stance that's way too wide for the shot they're playing.

When you have too much backswing and a stance width that's too wide, you're adding variables into a shot that really should be simple and not as complex as you might be making it. With the big backswing and a lateralshift across that wide stance from the lead foot to the trail foot, you'll end up with a long, large, decelerating movement instead of something shorter, more compact and accelerating through impact.

To complicate matters even more, many players make that big backswing and pull the club flat and to the inside—ruining the nice, simple, consistent swing plane that produces good shots. And since this is a short shot we're talking about, getting off plane like that is a big issue because there isn't as much time to recover as there would be on a full shot. The bigger swing is actually symptom of the bad swing plane, because players subconsciously realize that they need that time to try to manipulate the club to get it back on the right plane for solid contact.

With those mistakes, it's really hard to make consistently solid contact, and distance control becomes a matter of timing the swing perfectly. And all it takes is a few bladed and fatted shots in a row to really wreck your confidence. You get to the area of a hole where a good shot can really save your score and you're playing with the least amount of confidence—and creating even bigger scoring problems.

YES | PRE-SHOT ROUTINE: G.A.P.S (FOR EVERY SHOT YOU PLAY)

Take your GRIP with your arms parallel to the ground and plugged into your rib cage. Tilt forward from the hip joint as you AIM the club face to your start line, maintaining good POSTURE. Take your STANCE so that you are athletically balanced on the balls of your feet.

THE FIX

We'll get to the swing issues in a second, but I want to start by giving you the basic setup routine I teach at every Scoring Zone school. The best part about learning it is that it will work for your entire game—from driver to putter. I like to use the acronym GAPS—grip, aim, posture, stance—to form the basis of a simple, repeatable routine. That's key, because the vast majority of students I see come in with no routine at all. They set up differently from shot to shot and day to day, which means they have no idea of what's really working for them (and what isn't).

Start with G, your grip. How you hold the club for a variety of shots is an entire other book, but once you've set your hands on the club, stand behind the ball and choose your start line for the shot. Once you've picked that, turn perpendicular to that line and pull your shoulders back so that

your arms are resting on your ribcage. Now aim the clubface at a right angle to where you want the ball to go, while keeping your shoulders back and elbows "plugged in" to your ribcage. You've accomplished A, your aim.

Next, simply bend over and set the club on the ground by tilting from the hips. One way I describe it is to tilt forward with your chest while pushing your hips backward. If you've done it right, you'll be in terrific posture (the P). Your back won't be slumped or over arched. Make sure you have your weight equally balanced left to right and on the balls of your feet. Avoid the common tendency to set yourself back on your heels, which promotes a rising motion with the upper body in the backswing. From this stance (the S), you should feel like you can jump up in the air if you need to.

The order of your pre-shot routine is important. Most players make the mistake of setting their feet first and then adjusting their grip and alignment. You'll get a huge benefit if you set your grip first, then aim the face for your intended line, set your posture and finish with taking your stance so that you're on the balls of your feet (*previous page*).

Now let's talk about the particulars for this mini-wedge shot. The goal is to start with a setup that's a more appropriate base. If your feet would be shoulder-width apart for a full wedge shot, you want to move each of them about two inches toward the center for a half-shot—slightly wider for something longer and progressively narrower as the shot gets closer to the green.

With your base narrower, the next step is to work on making a pivot that stays between your feet, so to speak. On smaller shots like this, you are still going to load your weight to your trail side during the backswing, In fact, the shift we're talking about would be one that you couldn't even see—but you'll be able to feel it.

When you do it correctly, you're loading into your right quad and glute as you put pressure down through your right heel—while keeping your overall body position "inside" your foot. If you pictured an alignment aid coming up from the ground just inside your trail foot, your chest would not be moving beyond that imaginary line (*below*). With the narrower stance, it will take very little lateral movement to get back to your lead leg through impact and hold your finish.

The next step is to feel—and see—a good swing plane. On a shot of this size, you're looking for a swing that doesn't require you to have to manipulate the clubhead to produce a square impact. That means you don't

YES   MINI-WEDGE — NARROW BASE

With a narrow base load into your right (trail) hip so that you feel downward pressure on your right heel. Loading in the backswing makes it natural to unload and post into your left leg as the club swings down.

33

want to have to change the club's swing plane flatter or steeper during the swing, and you don't want to be forced to twist the face closed or hold it open.

If all of that sounds complicated to achieve, don't worry. Feeling it is probably simpler than you expect. Using the advice we just discussed about making a narrow, controlled pivot, make your backswing pivot and take the club back until your lead arm is parallel to the ground and the shaft is hinged at the wrist. From that position, let the club fall back to the ball without doing anything to change its path. If the sole of the club makes contact with the ground near the ball, you're doing great. If the back edge of the sole bottoms out behind the ball—which is the problem most players face—you're pulling the club back too flat. If the club comes down so that the leading edge digs into the ground behind the ball, your

YES ON PLANE

When the shaft is on plane, pointing at the ball in the back-swing, no adjustments need to be made on the downswing, just release the club head making solid and crisp contact with the ball.

plane is too steep. (You can think of the terms "flat" and "steep" as they relate to swing plane as the club's relative horizontal or vertical position. If the club is perpendicular to the ground, it is in a very steep position. If it is parallel to the ground, it is very flat). When the shaft is on a good plane, the butt of the club will be pointing at the ball you're trying to hit (*above*).

Once you've made a half dozen practice swings like this, you'll begin to see exactly where your club needs to go to in this halfway back position to be in the right place to go down cleanly to the ball. If all you do is practice finding this position and grooving that little pivot we discussed, the quality of your contact will improve dramatically.

THE NEXT STEP

One of the most common questions I get about mini-wedge shots is some variation of, "How do I know how hard to swing?"

Every player has to develop his or her own feel for distance, but there are certainly ways you can make that process easier and quicker. The simple act of making more solid contact is going to get you a good part of the way to better distance control—because you'll have a more consistent frame of reference for how far a certain swing hits a particular shot with a particular club.

As you start to change the speed at which you swing to change the distance you hit a shot, you have to pay attention to some particular problems this can bring. Some of the big problems we described earlier in this chapter come about because of the tendency to accelerate the club at the wrong time.

For example, if you used that too-big swing we discussed, you created the potential for more clubhead speed than you need for the distance you need to cover to get to the target. When that happens, you have two choices. You can can hit the ball too far, or you can decelerate the clubhead as it gets to the ball. Neither is a good outcome. You won't be able to make consistent, solid contact, and you won't have much distance control.

Acceleration is an important part of hitting quality mini-wedge shots, and modulating your speed is one way to fine tune the distance you hit a shot. But that acceleration should be coming down by the ball as the result of pivoting—as the end of a chain reaction that starts with your club. My friend Stan Utley likes to describe this feeling as one of throwing the clubhead through impact, and that's a visual that has proven to help people. I describe it as an act of constant, regulated acceleration—like putting your foot down smoothly on the gas pedal to go from the ramp to the highway. It's *not* like flooring it and spinning the tires in a burnout, then jamming on the brakes when you get to the stop sign.

When the club is on the right plane and you have a shorter distance to move it to get back to the ball—because you're no longer forced to reroute or otherwise manipulate it—you'll very quickly get the feel when it's time to push the accelerator smoothly and consistently through the ball (*next page*).

ADVANCED KNOWLEDGE

Once you've gotten good at the basic backswing-pivot-downswing combination I've been describing, you can start to add some different flavors to these shots to really get some precision. Some of that control comes in the form of changing the speed of your body and arm swing, but you have several other ways to adjust these shots.

The first and easiest way is to simply change the club you use. Many players have heard that picking a single club to hit for every short game shot is the "easiest" way to get a good feel for the short game. You can find some Tour greats who used that strategy for some great results, but when you have the kind of talent they do—and the time to practice—pretty much anything is possible.

I believe that learning to hit all different shades of shots with the same club is actually harder than learning a consistent motion and simply changing the tool you use with that motion. For example, if you have a 50-yard shot and need to hit a mini-wedge, you could certainly do that with your preferred short game club—say, a 56-degree sand wedge. But if you are comfortable with the movement we've been talking about, you can easily make the same shot with a 52-degree gap wedge or a lob wedge to either change the trajectory or the spin rate the ball takes to get to the target.

Once you've started to consistently hit solid mini-wedge shots, you can build an inventory of personal distances with your collection of wedges. With some practice, you can figure out how far a stock shot with your 56-degree wedge goes when you make a hip-height backswing, a shoulder-height backswing and a full backswing. Do the same with your other wedges and you've developed nine different specific "stock" dis-

YES | MINI-WEDGE SEQUENCE

Constant rate of smooth acceleration

As always,
start your mini
wedge shots by
STANDING TO THE
HANDLE.

With smooth acceleration allow the club to pull your body around so that your weight is solidly on your left (lead) leg.

tances with those clubs, along with a variety of trajectories.

On the course, it might unfold something like this. You might hit your sand wedge 40 yards with your hip-height backswing, and the same shot with your gap wedge might go 60 yards. When you have a 50-yard shot, you'd have the option to make a slightly smaller swing with the gap wedge or a slightly bigger swing with the sand wedge. You can then pick the right club for the situation. If you have a headwind and lots of green to work with, you might pick the lower lofted club. If you're at TPC Sawgrass and have to carry a lot of junk between you and the hole, the higher-trajectory shot would probably work better.

To make your own distance matrix, you'll need a rangefinder (personally, I'm a Bushnell man...) and a practice area where you can hit shots ranging from 40 to 80 yards. I actually like to do this exercise on the course late in the afternoon, when there isn't any play on the early holes, because then you can really get authentic conditions where you play. Some of my students even use an open field at a park, and drop towels down at various yardages. Go through a process with each wedge in your bag where you hit five shots with your hip-high swing and five with your shoulder-high swing.

With a gap wedge, sand wedge and lob wedge, you'll have clusters of balls at a variety of distances. Throw out any obvious outliers (blades, chunks) and average the remainder and you'll have a pretty good idea of what your "comfortable" yardages are. Ideally, you'll have a variety of distances covered with this exercise. After you have done the work you can come up with a mini wedge matrix. If you don't, it's time to change up your collection of wedges to provide better gapping. We're going to talk about that more in Chapter 5.

To watch players like Steve Stricker and Luke Donald hit these kinds of mini-wedge shots is to see how the body and arms work together to produce a smooth, consistent swing. They're not adding lots of extra speed by hinging the wrists in the backswing and unhinging them through the ball.

MINI WEDGE EXAMPLE MATRIX

	HIP HIGH	SHOULDER HIGH	FULL
Gap Wedge *(Low Trajectory)*	65	85	105
Sand Wedge *(Mid Trajectory)*	45	65	85
Lob Wedge *(High Trajectory)*	25	45	65

There are times when that hinging speed is useful—like when you need to play shots out of the sand or higher rough (which we're going to talk about in Chapter 5), or when you want to produce a lot more height—but it comes with the disadvantage of adding another variable to the shot. For the most part, you're going to get more consistent results if you swing with less wrist hinge and let the club approach the ball on a shallow angle instead of a steep one. The wrists move, but it's passive movement.

One of the big misconceptions about these off-speed shots from less-than-full yardages is that the best players are trying to create a lot of backspin to make the ball stop immediately. There might be some situations that call for a lot of backspin, but for the majority of "standard" mini-wedge shots, it's much more preferable—and more predictable—to make a "neutral" swing that flies the required distance because of the trajectory and size of swing you make. You definitely want to avoid the thought that you have to smash down on the ball aggressively to produce more spin. Your goal should be making a swing that lets the sole of the club skim the ground and make a shallow, straight mark on the grass. I hesitate to even call it a divot, because we're definitely not looking for a giant patch of turf to come flying out of there. It's a scrape, not a divot!

With some understanding of good technique and practice, you'll really be able to dial in these shots—and discover just how important they are to bringing down your score.

KEY POINTS — MINI-WEDGE

Setup

— Narrow your stance and play the ball just behind center.

Swing

— Stay centered during your backswing and finish on you forward leg.

— Swing the shaft on plane toward the ball.

— Work on "Hip to Hip" and "Shoulder to Shoulder" swings.

NOTES

CHAPTER 3

THE
PINCH SHOT

IF YOU CAME TO SEE ME outside Chicago for one of my full-day or two-day Scoring Zone schools, the first shot you would learn would be one I call the "Pinch Shot." Why call it the pinch shot instead of the common term "chip"? Because the idea here is that you are pinching the ball against the ground with the clubface, because the shaft is leaning forward.

It's an important one for a few reasons. First, it's a foundational shot for anybody's short game--one you can use in a variety of greenside situations. When you understand the mechanics of it, it's easy to pull off, and it's especially resistant to the nerves that can go with competing down the stretch, or just playing with friends.

Another reason why it's such a useful shot to learn is because of how closely the action through the ball mirrors what you do in a full swing. In the simplest terms, getting better at the pinch shot is going to help you with the quality of impact on all the rest of your shots.

Let's talk about what the pinch shot is, and where it fits in with the rest of the shots you might hit with less than a full swing. At the most basic level, a putting stroke is a one-lever, back-and-forth move—and one you could use if you wanted to from a good lie just off the green. A basic bump-and-run shot is essentially a putting stroke made with a lofted club like a middle iron, with the ball played slightly back of center.

When you get to the pinch shot (and, eventually, to the "high slider" shot we're going talk about in the next chapter), you're adding another lever to the swing to produce a little more speed and some height. Your body is still relatively quiet, like it is on a putt, but you're adding a slight lever of the wrists to the slight rotation of the shoulders.

Because the clubhead comes into the ball from the inside of the target line and hits the ball before the ground with the shaft slightly angled toward the target, the ideal pinch shot produces a lower ball flight, but it doesn't bound along the ground like a bump and run. For example, when used with a lob or sand wedge, it hits, then checks up and trickles to a stop. Because of this spin characteristic, the pinch shot is a very useful shot in a lot of situations where a player might not think a "low" shot would work.

One thing I want to point out right away is that "the Pinch Shot" doesn't mean low to the ground, like a bump and run. It means a shot with a lower trajectory than what would result from using the natural loft of the club. To pinch the ball, the shaft has to be leaning slightly forward, toward the target, which takes some of the natural loft off the face at impact. The result is a shot that flies lower than it normally would. When you do it right (and depending on the club you're using), it can be a fairly high shot that also has enough backspin to get the ball to stop fairly quickly when it hits the green. The club you use with this technique can change—and will affect the height of the shot. You could hit it with a pitching wedge and get a lower shot that rolls out more, or with a lob wedge and get a higher shot that checks and stops. The versatility of the shot makes it an important one to have in your short game arsenal.

THE PROBLEM

Let me give you an example to show you what I mean. Let's say you have a good lie in the fairway about 10 yards from the front edge of the green. The flag is another five yards onto the green--definitely in the front third (as opposed to the center or back third).

Even a single-digit player might look at this scenario and think that the best shot is some version of a high-lofted lob where you open the face and slide the club under and across the bottom of the ball. That's not a terrible play—and we're going to learn about how to hit those high sliders in the next chapter. It's just that it might be a higher-risk play than you really need for the situation.

But you can actually use the pinch technique with a more lofted club, like your 56- or 60-degree wedge, and produce a lower-flying shot that

YES · PINCH SHOT — DOWN THE LINE

Allow your chest to take the club back. Your arms should be passive going along for the ride, while your club-face stays pointed at the ball through the back-swing and impact.

uses some spin to check up near your target. It's actually an easier shot to hit than the high floater, and your results are more consistent if you hit one less than perfect.

Where a lot of players struggle is approaching this low shot with one of two big misconceptions. The first one is that they need to use a low-lofted club, like a 7- or 8-iron, move the ball back in the stance and hit down on the ball to produce a longer version of the bump and run we just talked about. This creates a situation where the club is coming down pretty steeply, and the leading edge is headed toward digging into the ground. Those irons also don't have enough loft on them to produce the right trajectory—which means that after seeing a few come out really low with too

much overspin, you'll tend to start to manipulate the loft on the clubhead to get the ball up in the air more or from going too far.

The other big misconception is that smaller shots like this are completely arms dominated. It's true that you don't want to make a whole big body turn on a short, pinch shot, but the thought you want to go with is that this motion is dominated by your chest. You're going to have some athletic freedom in your body instead of being rigid, but you're basically just making a small pivot and turning your chest while your arms swing at the same rate of speed as your torso. This is in contrast to the slider shot we'll talk about in the next chapter, where the upper body is more passive and the arms are responsible to swing the club.

In addition to the chest turn, you're going to use a slight wrist hinge. In the downswing, you'll release that hinge and the club will line up to where it was at setup. At impact, you'll have a straight line between the clubhead, hands, arms and body center.

THE FIX

To set up to the ball, you're going to use the handle of your wedge you've picked for the shot as your guide. Place the clubhead behind the ball so that the face is square to the target, the sole is flat on the ground and the handle is straight up and down—in other words, not pushed toward or away from the target.

Now, slightly shift the handle toward the target so it feels like your trail hand is over the ball. In measurement terms, this means the shaft is leaning about five or six degrees (about a ball width) toward the target. We're not talking about a giant shift like the ones many players make when they crank the handle hard toward the target—which has the effect of exposing the leading edge to the ground and encouraging it to dig in. It's a slight shift. Once you've set the handle, now set your feet and body so that the butt of the club is pointed toward your belt, and the the center of your chest, and your feet are six to eight inches apart. You'll now have the perfect ball position for this shot—which will be slightly back of center

The effect of standing to the handle this way will encourage you to have slightly more pressure on your lead leg at address—say, 60-40. This distribution is going to stay the same until right before impact, where you'll be 80-20. Unlike with a full shot, that requires shifting and the transfer of pressure back and forth, you're going to keep the pressure on your lead foot, make a small pivot, and hit this shot with a simple turn of your upper body.

As you take the club back, your focus should be on turning your chest to make the club move, letting your arms stay passive, and keeping the clubface pointing at the ball the way back and through to impact. You won't be making a huge swing—the clubhead will only get to about knee height for a 25-yard shot—so your hands won't get quite as high as your pockets.

By keeping the face pointed at the ball on the way back, you're encouraging a simple clubhead path that comes from the inside the target line and pinches the ball against the ground—and the loft of the club is going to do all the work you need to both produce height and create backspin. You don't need to add any release or extra hand action through impact to try to make that happen. Clean contact on the ball before the ground will take care of that for you.

As I emphasized in the previous chapter, the sequencing you use in the various short game shots is incredibly important. On this shot, the clubhead leads the way both back and through. It's what moves first in the backswing, and it's the thing that should start the downswing. Players really struggle when they start leading with their legs and driving them toward the target—which gets the club trailing behind the body with the face open. Then you have to use extra hand action to save the shot, and it gets ugly pretty fast.

Through impact, continue pivoting and turning your chest as you follow the clubhead to what will be a fairly low finish—lower than waist high in most cases. If at this point your weight has recoiled to your trail foot, you're doing too much with your lower body. Remember, the pressure distribution you set at address is what you want to keep until you're pivoting through impact. At that point, the pressure should increase to 80 percent on your lead leg and stay there through the finish (*next page*).

THE NEXT STEP

This small, simple movement is very straightforward, and 30 minutes of dedicated practice will get you feeling some very positive, crisp shots. You're going to want to keep an eye on a few common misses that can creep in—and as long as you know what you're looking for, you're going to be able to clean them up quickly.

One very common mistake is pulling the handle end of the club aggressively toward the target at the start of the downswing. This ruins the sequencing of the shot, and will tend to cause bladed and fat shots.

One way to beat this tendency is to use a little trick I've found works wonders. When you address the ball, start with a relatively relaxed grip

YES — PINCH SHOT — FACE ON

As always start at the set-up by STANDING TO THE HANDLE. Then keep the club-head in front of the body at all times during the swing.

pressure—at, say a 3 on a scale of 1-10. Just before you get to the hitting zone, increase that pressure to about a 6. The task of doing that will essentially distract your mind into getting more of the clubhead throw we want instead of pulling the handle toward the target. As you release the small lever created in the backswing, the clubhead accelerates through impact. The grip pressure increases to maintain a square clubface and solid contact.

The first thing you will discover as you start making clean contact consistently is that you'll quickly develop the ability to see the "standard" trajectory happening with the club you chose with this swing. When you can see the trajectory and you can start to predict the approximate area your ball will land, you're now training the important part of the tool—which is distance control.

There's no magic formula for getting better at hitting shots specific distances. It comes from seeing shot after shot hit at a certain "stock" speed and making that speed your baseline—then swinging faster or slower (or changing the wedge you use) to get a different distance. When you start identifying the landing spot that will produce the outcome you want, you'll be getting reinforced by many more positive results—balls ending up closer to the flag. There's a terrific way to practice this called the "last look." To make sure you're using your full powers of visualization and concentration on the correct goal, go through your entire pre-shot routine and set up process, then focus all of your attention on the specific landing spot where you want your ball to hit.

Before you pull the trigger on your swing, I want your last look to be at the specific landing spot—not the hole. If you make the hole your last look, your tendency is going to be to want to make a bigger swing to get the ball to that target, even subconsciously. Then, when you do swing, you'll make

DRILL   STORK DRILL—GREAT FOR ALL SCORING ZONE SHOTS!

a bigger backswing and have to slow the club down on the downswing to compensate. That's a recipe for deceleration and poor contact.

One question I get asked all the time is how to decide when to use this shot vs. the high slider we're about to talk about in the next chapter. If your technique is pretty good on the pinch shot—and you don't have some big obstacle in front of you to carry—you'll be able to use this pinch shot on at least 80 percent of the short game scenarios you face. It's ideal when you have a flag in the middle or back third of the green and have some room to land in front of the target, but you can also adapt it to a pin that's more in front.

One thing you do have to have for this shot is a clean lie—either in the fairway or in a light cut of rough where there's no grass between the back of the ball and your club. You need to be able to pinch the ball with the

The Stork Drill is my favorite drill—with your trail leg pulled back, your knees touching and your trail heel lifted off the ground, you are naturally encouraged to rotate your upper body over your lead leg as the club strikes the ball.

club, and if you get grass in between you'll either produce a no-spin flyer or dig the club and barely move the ball.

ADVANCED KNOWLEDGE

Two big killers in the short game are L-words: Lateral and Lag. If you get a lot of lateral body motion, or you pull the handle instead of moving the clubhead, you're going to struggle a lot. This basic drill called the "stork drill" will really help you erase both of those issues and hit wonderful pinch shots.

Set up in the way we've just been describing the pinch shot, but before you hit a shot, pull your trail foot back and lift the heel so that you're on the toe of that foot. Now, hit some shots where you focus on keeping your chest rotating as the clubhead accelerates through the shot. With only one

On the pinch shot, focus on where you want the ball to land (*above, left*) vs. where you want the ball to end up (*above right*).

foot flat on the ground, you won't be able to make any of that lateral motion. The turning of your chest over your lower body, will keep your weight firmly planted over your lead leg as the club stays in front of your body. (*previous page*).

To build a basic strategy for playing this shot, break the green into three 10-yard segments. The goal is always to land the ball somewhere in the front segment of the green. If the pin is in the front segment, use your lob wedge. If it's in the second segment, use your sand wedge. If it's in the back segment, use your gap wedge. If you should run into a really big green, keep breaking it into 10-yard segments and add one club per 10-yard increment. For a 50-yard deep green, you'd use your 9-iron to land the ball in the front segment and roll it to the back (*above*).

KEY POINTS — THE PINCH SHOT

Setup

— Lean the shaft toward the target.

— Stand to the Handle.

— Stance 6-8 inches, weight center or just forward.

Swing

— Club-face stays toward the ball.

— Upper body makes a slight pivot, while arms go along for the ride.

— Club-head initiates downswing followed by upper body, then lower body.

— Weight ends up on the forward leg, club head finishes under the belt line.

NOTES

NOW THAT YOU'VE GRADUATED from the pinch shot, it's time to build on those skills and take them to the next logical place—to what I call the "high slider." I call it a high slider because I want you to envision the club-head sliding under the bottom of the ball.

The high slider is exactly what it sounds like. It's a shot that spends more time in the air than along the ground, which makes it very useful when you need to clear rough or some other obstacle in front of you, carry to an elevated tier on a green, or stop the ball more quickly when you don't have a lot of green to work with.

A lot of the players who come to see me for a short game school have an interesting relationship with lofted greenside shots. If you watch a lot of PGA Tour golf on television, you see players using a lofted option a lot around the green—to the point that it seems like it's the only kind of shot they hit. But the conditions at tour events dictate what shot makes the most sense to play. A lot of times, super firm conditions and fast greens demand something with a lot more air time—especially for players at the level where saving par is a must to make the cut and compete on the weekend.

What does this have to do with you?

Because so many players see the best players using lofted greenside shots played with a relatively high amount of clubhead speed, they tend to try to use that shot a lot in their own game. Don't get me wrong. It's really important to understand how to hit a high slider—and we're going to talk about how to do that in this chapter. But it's also important to understand that sometimes it isn't the best choice for the situation at hand if you aren't playing tournament golf for a living.

My goal here is to help you understand not only *how* to hit a consistent, effective high slider, but *when* to choose that shot instead of the pinch shot we talked about in the last chapter. By picking the most favorable conditions to hit each shot, your confidence level will go up—which will also increase your chances of hitting a good shot.

THE PROBLEM

This won't be the first time you've heard this, but your instincts are actually making it harder for you to hit a well-executed high-lofted shot. Intuitively, it *feels* right to try to help the ball in the air with your body and your hands. And the most common mistake players make when they try to hit a standard high toss shot is to hang back with the upper body. The trail shoulder dips closer to the ground as the upper body falls back toward the back leg. The player then usually tries to use the hands to try to add loft onto the club and scoop the ball into the air. It feels like what you should be doing to toss something with some height.

But the reality is very different. On a good shot, you're actually going to do the opposite. When a student comes to me with this hanging back issue, I'll usually start with a simple visual. I'll hold a shaft about six inches off the ground a foot in front of them (toward the target), and I'll ask them to try to hit a tiny little shot under the shaft. Almost every time, they'll make a natural adjustment to feel what to them is hitting down on the ball to make it go lower.

The result? The ball pops up into the air, thanks to the natural loft already on the clubface. The point here, is there is a natural tendency to help the ball into the air, when what we need to do is learn to strike down and through the ball allowing the loft of the chosen club to do it's job, lifting the ball into the air.

So what we're after here is a basic setup and combination of techniques that will get you to deliver the club with a slightly descending blow and a predictable, neutral clubface that lets the natural loft send the ball up into the air. The adjustments you make relative to the pinch shot we just learned will automatically bake in this increased speed and height.

YES HIGH SLIDER — DOWN THE LINE

For high slider, swing the club up with your arms and hands keeping the body passive. Notice how the clubface stays open through impact into the finish.

THE FIX

First, let's talk about the difference between your setup for the high slider and the set up for the pinch shot. On the pinch shot, we started with some slight shaft lean toward the target (which reduces the effective loft on the face and sets up a lower trajectory).

For the slider, the handle should be neutral (perpendicular to the ground) and the face either square to the target or slightly open (*page 62*). Similar to the pinch shot, you then set your stance in relationship to that shaft by standing to the handle so that it's pointing at the center of your chest, with your feet about six to eight inches apart. This sets the ball just forward of center in your stance, vs. the back-in-the-stance position for the pinch shot. Another clear difference is the clubface rotates open so that the leading edge is pointing up (*above*).

From this starting position, you'll make a swing that is fundamentally different than the one you used for the pinch shot. Where the pinch shot is controlled by the upper body with the arms and hands going along for the ride, the slider is much more of an arms-and-hands controlled shot. You're making a longer, softer arm swing to produce the speed you need to slide the club through the grass under the ball and produce speed and spin.

When you make this arms-dominated swing, you're going to be adding some wrist hinge during the backswing and letting that hinge go through impact so that the clubhead and hands create a straight line at the point of impact (*page 63*). I've heard teachers and players describe this hinging and unhinging as throwing the clubhead, but to me it feels more like a softer "catch up" of the clubhead to the hands. When you hinge your wrists, you're creating an angle between the shaft and your lead arm, and when the club catches up, it means that angle has gone back to where it was at address. Sometimes I use the phrase with students—"Catch up, firm up"—meaning the club catches up to the hands as the hands firm up on the grip.

YES HIGH SLIDER — FACE ON OFF A TIGHTER LIE

Off a tighter lie, limit your wrist action and primarily use your arms to swing the club back. Swing the clubhead back down realigning the club to the body center.

Even though this is a relatively short greenside shot, how you move your body and transfer your weight is extremely important. As we talked about above, the fundamental problem many players have with this shot is hanging back and scooping. And some of the advice you may have heard about how to hit this shot could be contributing to that problem.

Because it's important to have your pressure shifted onto your lead foot at impact, some teachers will suggest starting at address with your weight already favoring your lead side at, say, 60-40. But from what I've seen, that tends to encourage many players to make a bigger shift back in the backswing--which produces an even more exaggerated hang back move.

I'd prefer you to start with a narrow, balanced stance where your pressure is spread evenly—50-50—over both feet. As you swing back and through, feel as though you're making a very slight centered rotation of your upper body over a stable lower body. Remember this is predominately an arms-and-hands controlled swing. You shift your pressure gently toward your back foot, then shift forward through impact. It's a subtle pressure change—not a dramatic shift back and forth. It's the same feeling you'd get if you were pitching pennies or tossing a ball underhanded toward a target down range. You're moving with gravity, instead of locking yourself in place unnaturally. I want to re-emphasize the point I made in Chapter 1 about sequencing. It's so important to get the clubhead starting down first, followed by the rotation of the upper body over

YES **HIGH SLIDER — FACE ON FROM DEEP ROUGH**

Compared to the backswing position on page 62, you can clearly see more wrist hinge is needed to steepen the angle of descent when the ball is nestled down in the rough. Finish on your left side.

the lead hip. You want to get your weight so that it's solidly over your lead side, not falling backward (*previous page*).

THE NEXT STEP

Because of the wrist hinge and speed that's a basic part of this shot, it's one that is pretty versatile. When you have a tighter lie keep your wrist passive which will allow the club to descend but on a shallower angle, (like a plane landing). When the ball is down in the rough, the more wrist hinge and more speed you're going to need to use, so the clubhead is descending on the steeper angle (like a plane crashing) The high slider out of deep rough is much like the bunker-rough-explosion shot we're going to talk about in the next chapter (*above*).

When exactly should you use the high slider? For the low handicappers

I teach, it works out to be about a third of the short game shots they hit—which means that the default play in many cases is the pinch shot. If you have a handicap higher than 10, I'd suggest only using this shot about 10 to 15 percent of the time, and only when there's a cushion of grass under the ball. When the turf is firm, it increases your chance of blading the shot and bringing a big number in play. If you're in doubt, the pinch shot is a better choice, with more room to make a mistake and still hit a decent shot.

The most obvious scenarios for the high slider are when you have to clear something in front of you to get to the green—a bunker, a wide expanse of rough, or some other hazard—or when you need to be able to carry the ball to a specific part of the green or to take a bunch of undulation or tiering out of play. The high slider is useful when the flag is on a lobe of the green with not much flat space around the hole to work with—because the trajectory and spin will let you reduce the distance the ball will run out.

If your basic technique is solid, you don't have to make any adjustments for the tightness of the lie--even if it feels like you're going to blade it from a lie that's very thin and firm. The bounce on the bottom of the club is designed to skid along the ground, if you don't pull on the handle and keep your hinge too long, you'll get a decent result. Even on less-than-perfect contact, you'll most likely end up on the green looking at a 20-footer— which is much better than trying to recover from blading the ball over the green, because you made the common mistake of hanging back trying to lift the ball into the air instead of trusting the loft of the club to do its job. On the course, pick the shot you feel confident in, and at the practice range work on the less confident ones. In time, you'll have more scoring choices for every situation.

ADVANCED KNOWLEDGE

Once you start to get the feel for this shot and have relatively repeatable control of impact, you want to be able to translate that predictability onto the course itself. That means being able to visualize the trajectory of the shot you're about to play and pick the landing area where the shot will hit--and how far it will run out. One major adjustment players begin to make as they get better is that they stop seeing the flag as the target. After all, there's going to be run out after your ball lands, just like you learned in the pinch shot chapter, focus on where you want the ball to land and not where you want it to end up.

One of the common questions I get at this point is about club selection. If you're visualizing a landing point that's farther away, or if you want to change the trajectory of the shot, do you hit this shot with a different club? It's not really as complicated as it might seem. In the most basic terms, I use my lob wedge for most shots from good lies in the fairway, and my sand wedge set slightly open from the rough.

I like the simplicity of using the same club and making some subtle adjustments to produce the shot I want, unlike the pinch shot when I'm changing clubs to change the trajectory and rollout of the golf ball. If you're looking for more height, you can shift the handle of the club so that it is leaning slightly away from the target at address, open the face a little more—or do both. These adjustments will produce plenty of height with a 54-56 degree club out of the rough and a 58-60 degree club out of the fairway, to the point that you wouldn't need any more even on the hardest, fastest greens in the world.

To play a longer shot, you can make the opposite adjustment. Move the shaft just slightly less than vertical, and instead of opening the face play it square. Now you can adjust the distance of the shot by making a larger swing. In any case, the longest distance you'll want to cover with this technique is about 25 yards of carry distance. After that, it becomes a mini-wedge shot, like we discussed in the first chapter.

KEY POINTS— HIGH SLIDER

Setup

— Set the shaft perpendicular to the ground.

— Stand to the Handle.

— Stance 6-8 inches, weight centered.

Swing

— Clubface opens as the club swings back.

— Arms and hands swing the club up while body stays passive.

— Weight ends up on the forward leg, clubhead finishes close to shoulder height.

NOTES

CHAPTER 5

BUNKER PLAY

FOR A LOT OF PLAYERS, everything changes when they get into the bunker. Stance. Grip. Ball position. How open the face is. The kind of swing. The expectation level for a good result. All of it changes.

When we get to that part of the game in one of my one-day schools, I'll watch a small group of students go through all of the different adjustments and contortions to hit sand shots their way, then tell them something that usually comes as a big surprise.

You don't have to change much to be a good bunker player.

In fact, if all you do is use the skills we just talked about for the high slider (and add a lot of clubhead speed), you'll become much more consistent out of the sand. Instead of looking at the bunker as a place where double bogies are born, you'll see them as chances to get up and down.

I understand why all the adjustments are happening for most players when they get in the sand. They've heard all of the instruction chatter about how to hit a good sand shot—and maybe have even had a lesson. They've heard that you need to open the face and stance dramatically, hit two inches behind the ball, throw the sand out, etc., etc. And they've also heard over and over from the commentators how easy bunker shots are for tour players to hit, and how they actually prefer to play from the sand over rough.

Why is it that there's so much difference between players who make bunker play look so easy and those who are terrified when they see their approach shot headed for the sand?

As always, it starts with setup. Bad bunker players usually make it harder than it has to be to get out of the sand. They're adding angles and adjustments in their setup that force them into compensations right away, and then compound that by adding way too much lateral movement in the swing itself. With the right setup and a basic understanding of how to make the bottom of the club work through the sand, you can actually hit almost anywhere behind the ball and produce a decent shot. With good technique, getting the ball out is simple—once you can get the ball out consistently, you can start to focus your attention on getting it close to the hole.

THE PROBLEM

At the most basic level, players with bunker issues see sand shots as fundamentally different than regular pitch shots from the rough. In reality, they're no different, other than more clubhead speed is needed. Yes, the ball is sitting in a different lie, on a different kind of surface, and the idea that you don't actually hit the ball itself can play tricks on the mind. Players tend to open their stance dramatically, and open the face of the club by putting their hands forward instead of opening the face of the club and *then* setting their grip. As a result, the ball ends up very back in the stance, and the only way to hit it is to hang back to try to scoop the ball out of the sand. Even if you hit it out of the sand, you don't have the loft or speed through the ball to make the shot fly high with good spin. You can't control the shot.

Another common issue? When you start driving your lower body toward the target to gain enough speed to try to "explode" the ball on a cushion of sand, you screw up the two main fundamentals that apply to bunker shots. You don't want lateral motion, and you want to preserve loft on the face.

Moving laterally—shifting your lower body toward the target as you start the downswing—usually has the effect of reducing the loft on the

NO CLUBHEAD DIGGING VS. SLIDING

When the hands lead the clubhead digs into the sand, losing the necessary loft and speed to get the ball into the air and carry it far enough.

club. The handle leads the head through impact, which both reduces loft and makes the leading edge dig into the sand. Once you dig in too much and fail to move the ball, you'll start to subconsciously adjust on the downswing by moving laterally at first, then tilting and hanging back as you throw your hands to try to save the shot (*above and right*).

All of these adjustments make it impossible to consistently hit the sand in the same place with the right amount of loft on the face and the glide—the back edge of the sole of your sand wedge—skidding through the sand instead of digging. You've heard wedge manufacturers call this back edge of the wedge sole the "bounce," but I like to call it the "glide," because

YES BUNKER SET-UP, SIMPLE 1-2-3

1.

2.

that term helps players visualize the club gliding through the sand—not bouncing off it.

THE FIX

Let's start with the idea that this isn't some foreign shot that requires a big change in technique. The fundamentals are very similar to a high slider— with more clubhead speed to account for the resistance of the sand. Your goal is to make the glide on the back of the wedge slide through the sand, and the only way to do that is getting the clubhead to get to the ball before the grip.

You can get 70 percent of the way there with a good setup.

As you look at the club, set the leading edge open to 1:00, then take your grip. Set the shaft perpendicular to your target line, then STAND TO THE HANDLE.

Begin with your regular grip for a distance wedge with the face square to the target. Turn the leading edge slightly open (to 1:00 on the face of the clock, if 12:00 is square), then take your grip again. Next, line up the shaft so it is perpendicular to your target line. As with every other shot we've discussed, **stand to the handle**. Your feet will be as wide apart as they would be for a shot with a 7-iron. When you stand to the handle, the ball will be slightly forward of center, and your weight will be distributed 50-50 across both feet. Dig your feet into the sand approximately a half inch—which should be consistent with the depth of the divot your club-head will make. Your chest will be square to slightly open to the target line, something I watched Bill Harmon teach his students years ago from

YES | BUNKER SHOT — DOWN THE LINE

fundamentals he learned from his father, Claude Harmon. Opening your chest too much in the setup (a common mistake) sets your chest in front of the ball, which discourages you from turning your upper body through on the downswing. If you don't turn your chest through, you'll stall out and hang back—a bunker shot killer.

At this point, you might be wondering why you shouldn't cheat your weight toward your lead foot. It's a common tip you'll hear from a lot of short game teachers, because they believe that beginning with your weight favoring your lead side will make it easier for it to stay there during the shot. I've found the opposite to be true. If you start with too much pressure on your lead foot, the tendency is to fall backward as the club swings forward in an effort to keep the clubhead from slamming deeply into the sand. As with every short game shot, if the clubhead is bottoming out too soon

It's OK to be slightly open to the target just not wide open. Swing the clubhead higher with your hands so that you will have enough speed to get the ball out on a cushion of sand.

YES   BUNKER SHOT — FACE ON

My weight stays centered through the backswing, which helps me maximize my arm swing. This produces the club-head speed I need to get through the sand. I finish on my lead leg.

YES — CLUBHEAD PROPERLY GLIDING THROUGH THE SAND

With a good bunker technique the shaft comes back to neutral so that the back edge of the clubhead is able to slide through the sand —throwing the ball out.

and moving upward through impact, you're going to have a lot of problems.

From this address position, you're stable and ready to swing with some speed from your hands and arms. I stress hands and arms because you don't want your body to be actively involved in the backswing, which helps keep the club in front of your body. It is extremely important to follow the advice we talked about in the last chapter about shifting—namely, that you want to stay very centered. I want you to have passive shoulders, upper body and legs in the backswing, and swing your arms high enough to create the vertical speed you'll need to get the clubhead through the ball.

Clubhead glides through the sand.

According to a television segment I watched from Cameron McCormick Jordan Spieth's coach, Jordan's clubhead speed on a greenside bunker shot is between 60 to 70 miles per hour. That's a lot of speed for a short club on a short shot! (*page 78*).

What does this feel like from the top of the backswing? Your weight should feel centered over both feet, like at address. The clubhead starts everything down to the ball, as a kind of throwing move. The arms and upper body respond to the throw, and the legs just come along for the ride as the club makes its way through the sand. You're not frozen over the ball. Your body simply responds to what your arms are doing (*pages 78-81*).

Instead of all the crazy adjustments and angles you previously worried about out of the sand, I just want you to think about one thing. Get the club into the sand before the ball so that your hands and your body center all make a straight line. The head will slightly lead the hands through impact, and you'll be creating loft and using the glide.

When you do it right, the club enters the sand three or four inches behind the ball, but doesn't dig. It skims along just under the surface, and you make an eight or 10-inch long divot that is consistently about a half inch deep. The wider part of the divot should be in front of the ball, not behind it—which is an indicator that you're getting through the shot and not hanging back. The club makes a crisp slapping sound in the sand, and you don't feel a tremendous amount of resistance.

How far is three inches behind the ball? You could lay a folded dollar bill down just behind the ball and hit at the far edge of it and be fine. It's plenty of room. You could miss your intended entry spot by an inch either way and still hit a perfectly acceptable shot. Just that knowledge will free you to let the club swing, because you know you don't have to be perfectly precise. There's a fairly large margin of error as long as you are going forward and not falling backward.

THE NEXT STEP

The basic motion won't be hard for you to pick up with a bit of practice. Even if you don't make any other adjustments to account for the distance of the shot you have in front of you, making this vanilla, stock swing will get you out of the bunker and on the green—which, for a lot of players, is a huge improvement.

After you have conquered the basics, you're going to want to know how to adjust your technique to account for different distances. You do this with swing speed and club selection.

For the vanilla shot we just learned, your basic clubhead speed ratio is going to be at least double what you would use for a shot of similar distance from a normal lie in light rough. For heavy sand or a buried lie, you'll have to swing even faster—all the way up to three times the speed.

Your instinct will probably tell you to worry about hitting the ball too far, but that shouldn't be a huge concern if your technique is decent. The more speed you produce, the higher you'll hit the ball, and the more spin you'll tend to make. Even if a shot goes too far, the higher trajectory and increased spin will limit the damage.

Make sure you have a big enough arm swing to have plenty of time to produce sufficient speed. You're going to want to get your hands up at least as high as your shoulders. It will probably feel a little strange at first, but the big arm swing will really reduce your natural urge to use a lot of lower body to generate clubhead speed. Once you know you have enough swing size to get through the sand, it becomes much easier to relax and swing the clubhead.

Once you've worked on the stock swing speed for a basic bunker shot of, say, 15 yards, you can start to make some subtle adjustments to go shorter and higher or longer. Instead of swinging slower for a shorter shot, you can open the face of your sand wedge a little more in the setup phase—to, say, 2:00—or you can switch to your lob wedge with the leading edge set at 1:00. For a longer shot, you can swing harder, or you can move down to a gap wedge and do everything we just described.

Just keep in mind that simplicity is your friend. Get really good at the stock bunker shots with your three wedges—and knowing the distances those shots go—before you start doing a lot of experimenting. Make sure you're getting out of the bunker, even if you're left with a longer putt. I like to tell my students over and over, "protect the bogey."

ADVANCED KNOWLEDGE

With all this new information about your sand game, you're probably ready to go out and take on the world. That's great, but first make sure the clubs you have are going to make the job as easy as possible.

The default loft option for a sand wedge is 56 degrees, and that might end up being a great loft for you. But there are some details that are important to check out along the way. Your first stop should be checking the loft on your pitching wedge. A lot of new sets come with pitching wedges that are 45 or 46 degrees, which means that your sand wedge shouldn't really be the next wedge in your bag unless you're OK with a pretty substantial gap on both full shots and around the green.

I like to set my students up with consistent loft gaps between their wedges. For example, if you have a 45-degree pitching wedge, your set of wedges should include a 50-degree gap wedge, a 55-degree sand wedge and a 60-degree wedge. Another combination could be 46-50-54-58.

I'm not a big fan of 56-degree sand wedges, because the loft on a standard pitching wedge has gotten much stronger over the years. That means your gap wedge should be closer to 50 degrees. The bottom line is that you need to know what your pitching wedge loft is, and work from that in four or five degree increments.

The next most common question I get is about the "bounce" wedges are built with. As I mentioned earlier, "bounce" isn't my favorite term. I like to call it glide. Whichever term you use, we're talking about the degree to which the back edge of the wedge is lower than the leading edge. You might see that your sand wedge has as much as 12 degrees of bounce, while your lob wedge might have only six to nine degrees. In general terms, the more bounce a club has, the more glide is built in on the bottom edge of the head. A club with more bounce will slide more instead of dig. That can be useful in the sand, but a pain in the neck if you play a lot of firm courses with tight grass. A club with a lot of bounce will literally bounce off the turf.

If you improve your technique with the tips in this chapter, the amount of bounce on the bottom of your clubs isn't going to matter as much. Even a low bounce club like a lob wedge (or a pitching wedge) has plenty of glide to work in normal bunker sand with this technique. Personally, I like to have a sand wedge with ten to 12 degrees of bounce, and a lob wedge with a lower bounce, more like six degrees. That way, you have a wedge in your bag that's suited to thick sand, heavy rough, as well as tight lies or whatever other situation you might encounter.

The grind a wedge has—where the actual bounce material is situated—is just important to me than the total amount of bounce. For example, some wedges are ground so that the glide on the bottom is less substantial near the heel, so the club is easier to play when it's open. The word grind itself actually comes from the tour, where players got the characteristics they were looking for by using an actual grinder to remove metal from the bottom of a stock wedge. You don't need to overthink this part of the game, but I do believe it's useful to have a lob wedge with a grind that features less metal on the heel. This makes it easier to open the face when you want to hit a higher shot.

With the right equipment, setup and technique, all you need is some time and practice and you'll actually be excited to play your next bunker shot out on the course.

KEY POINTS — EXPLOSION/BUNKER

Setup

— Set the face open to 1:00 or 2:00 o'clock, depending on desired height and needed distance.

— Grip the club after the clubface is set.

— Align the shaft perpendicular to the intended start line.

— Stand to the Handle.

— Stance is shoulder width, dig into the sand about a 1/2. "

Swing

— Clubface stays open as the arms and hands swing the club up.

— Hands swing as high as the shoulder line.

— Body stays passive and centered.

— Swing the clubhead down with speed, so the the clubhead glides through the sand on it's back edge.

— Weight finishes on forward leg.

NOTES

CHAPTER 6

DRILLS AND PRACTICE

THE SHORT GAME is a place where you have almost unlimited creative options to solve the problem in front of you. Those choices make this part of the game so interesting—and can be potentially fun—to learn.

What I hope you've discovered over the course of reading this book is that those creative options are all built with a relatively short list of short game fundamentals. Those fundamentals are the handful of key ingredients you can combine in different ways to produce different shots.

In this chapter, I want to review with you those crucial fundamentals, give you my list of "anti-fundamentals"—things that are certified short game killers—and cover some of the ways you can make your practice time more productive.

No matter what style differences you have throughout your short game, I consider the following to be the ultimate list of "do's" or critical fundamentals that are required to produce high-quality, consistent contact. When you can hit the ball solidly the same way almost every time for the shot you're trying to hit, you get really confident about your distance control—and about your technique in general.

How do you hit it great?

1. The clubhead needs to be descending through impact, regardless of the shot you want to hit (*right*). This is true for the high slider, pinch shot and explosion shot from the fairway bunker or heavy greenside rough.

CLUBHEAD DESCENDING

YES

When the clubhead descends through impact (*above*), the ball flies into the air, as compared to the ascending skulled and chunked shots below.

SKULLED SHOT

NO

CHUNKED SHOT

NO

YES   SHAFT LEAN IN RELATION TO TARGET—PINCH SHOT, HIGH SLIDER AND BUNKER

2. Always set the handle first, then stand to it. If you only remember one thing from this book, Stand to the Handle (STH) would be the one thing I hope you take away. If you have a general idea of how the shaft should be leaning in relation to the target, you have a great guide to get your body in the right place to start a swing. For a pinch shot, the handle leans slightly toward the target. For a high slider or bunker shot, the handle moves to vertical or even leaning slightly away from the target. Then you set your body so that the handle is pointing at the center of your sternum. Your ball position is then set almost automatically (*above*).

3. Use the finesse downswing sequence. When making a finesse swing for these short game shots we've been discussing, the clubhead needs to start the downswing, followed by the upper body. The lower body moves last, and only in response to what the upper body is doing (*next page*).

Always set the shaft in relation to the Target first,
then Stand To The Handle.

YES · TOP-DOWN SEQUENCING (CLUBHEAD FIRST)

4. Increase your grip pressure through impact. Set a lighter grip pressure at the start, then increase tension as you go down through the ball (*pages 96-97*).

On the other side of the coin, there are a few things you absolutely don't want to do in short game.

Here are the killers.

1. If the club is moving upward through impact, you've either hit way behind it (fat, chunk), or you've hit the ball thin or skulled it. Even if you make just a slight mistake here, the loss of solid contact really affects your distance control.

2. Getting the handle out of alignment at address. When you push the handle dramatically toward the target at address—and have it pointed forward of the center of your body—you're creating a scenario where the

The clubhead leads, with the upper body following and the lower body responding. When done properly your weight should end up on your left (lead) leg with the club in front of you.

Right: Setting the handle forward and the body back is a sure way to chunk or skull the shot!

NO LOOSE HANDS

A loose grip at impact results in loss of club-head control!

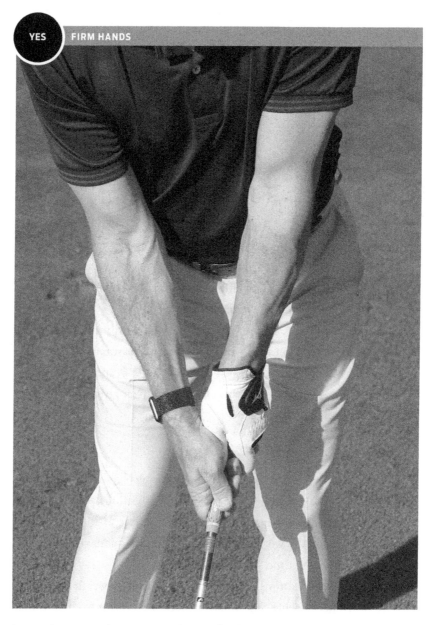

YES FIRM HANDS

Increasing your grip pressure at impact leads to solid contact
and club-head control!

upper body tilts back and the bottom of the swing is set up to happen too far behind the ball. You're basically eliminating all of the technology built into the wedge and making it way more likely to chunk, blade or dig the leading edge of the club into the ground.

3. Using the power downswing sequence (*left*). If you set up and swing like you're hitting a full shot, you're going to generate way too much speed for these small shots. That means a wide stance and a downswing initiated by lower body drive is going to cause you lots of problems. This sequence creates too much clubhead lag in the downswing—something you don't want.

4. Grip tension. Most players grip the club too tightly at address, and then loosen when they get to the ball. Tight grip pressure from the start makes your arms and shoulders tense and keeps you from making a good finesse sequence. Loose grip pressure through impact gives you less control over the clubhead.

YOUR PRACTICE PLAN

I use the word "plan" very intentionally, because the biggest problem I see with most players is that even if they have good intentions about working on their short game—and they actually spend the time to go work on it— they don't approach the work with a plan. Without a plan, you won't get the most use out of the time.

I had the honor of sitting in on one of Mike Kryzyzewski's basketball practices at Duke. Coach K had the time organized down to the minute. Practice was broken down into 10 to 15 minute segments, so the players could have intense focus on one skill before moving on to the next element. Even the rest breaks were planned out and timed.

Take a page from Coach K's book and segment your practice the same way. Let's say you have an hour to practice, you want to break the game into segments, and spend 20 minutes on putting, 20 on short game and 20 on your full swing.

Within that 20 minutes of short game practice, how should you allocate your time? Use the same segmented concentration. You want to be practicing each of the different shots we learned here—mini-wedge, pinch shot, high slider and bunker shot) in its own segment of time. But instead of breaking the time down equally between those four shots, you want to spend more of your time on the shots you have the least confidence in on the course.

For example, let's say you're weakest at hitting the high slider or bunker shot. I do want to emphasize that the pinch shot is the most important because it is the most used shot. You need to be confident at it, so make it a priority. When you get to your 20 minutes of short game practice time, that's the first place you need to go and spend time. When it comes to practicing the shots you're the best at, you want to be honing your skills—looking at challenges that encourage you to improve how close you can get to the hole.

Putting is a whole other world—and one we're going to cover in a *Putting Zone* book—but in general, that part of your practice should be about getting better at the skills you need on the course. Most players find a spot about 10-15 feet from the hole and hit a bunch of the same putts over and over again. But on the course, long putts of more than 30 feet and short ones from 4-6 feet are going to be the ones that impact your score the most. If you can consistently lag long putts near the hole and have a better approach for making the short ones, you're going to have a decent putting day (*next page*).

If you don't have time to separate your short game and putting practice,

DRILL LAG PUTTING AND 9-BALL PUTTING

Practice lag putting from 30-60 feet to reduce your number of 3-putts.
Practice from 4-6 feet to convert your up and downs on all the Scoring Zone
shots, which is the whole point of this book.

you can play the 9-Shot game to get a full short game work out. Drop nine
balls in various lies and distances around the green, and play out each one.
Hit the shot, then putt out from where you end up. If you never get up and
down from any of the lies, your score would be 27 or worse. If you do it
every time, you'd score 18. What scores do you consistently shoot? Are you
trending downward? Which shots give you the most trouble? And is your
putting masking some of the problems you might be having on particular
short shots? (*pages 102-103*).

BEFORE YOU PLAY
The time before a round is a lot different than independent practice time.

DRILL 9-SHOT SCORING ZONE GAME

Place nine balls around the green in all different scenarios to test your skills. For each one, keep score of how many shots it takes you to get up and down. Improve your average score and you'll improve your game.

At the conclusion of any short-game shot, you should be able to lift your trail leg if all your weight is balanced on your forward leg. Then pull the club into the center of your body.

Before you play, you don't want to be in construction mode, trying to change around your fundamentals. It's a time to find some good feels that will work for you that day.

Most players get ready to play by hitting a bunch of drivers, a few 7-irons and then some putts on the practice green. They're not ready to play. They miss the first green, hit a bad chip and get off to a bad start when they didn't have to.

I like to get to the course early enough that I can spend 15 minutes on each segment—full swing, short game and putting. In full swing, I'll start with some wedges and work my way through every other club to the driver, then finish by visualizing and hitting the shot I'm going to need on the first tee.

DRILL THE STORK DRILL IS THE BEST SHORT-GAME DRILL

The Stork Drill works for all Scoring Zone shots because it helps a player to lead the down swing with the club-head and finish with the weight on the lead leg.

DRILL CLIP-THE-TEE DRILL

The Clip-The-Tee drill is a great drill to help you learn to control of the bottom of your golf swing. Once you can clip a tee on its own, put a ball on it and continue focusing on the tee and not lifting the ball into the air.

When I get to the short-game area, I hit a variety of shots—tight lies, thick lies—with the goal of simulating what I expect to see on the course. I'll also make sure to hit a few bunker shots to get a sense for the sand. A lot of players don't do that, but you may go a few rounds without hitting a sand shot, and if you don't warm up with some, the first one could be terrible.

This is the time to feel your short game shots and get a sense for what's working and what isn't. If you go through this pre-round circuit and see that your high slider shots just aren't working, practice the "stork" you learned in chapter three for the pinch shot. This drill is my favorite because it actually works for any of *The Scoring Zone* shots in this book including the bunker explosion. Just go through the same set up for a pinch shot, and with your feet close together, pull your right foot back so that the ball of your right foot is in line with your left arch. Go up on your right toe, stand to the handle and make some practice swings. If you hang back at all, you'll lose your balance. Your weight also needs to stay centered during the swing for this stance to work. You can either use this as a practice swing feel and go back to your regular stance, or you can even use it to hit real shots. To see if a player has turned through properly, a great check point I like to use is to have a player lift their trail leg then pull the club into the stomach (*page 105*).

Sometimes you just need to stop the bleeding!

We're at the end of *The Scoring Zone*, and I'm excited to hear about how your game is progressing. Visit my website at **ToddSones.com** and send me a message, and sign up to learn about our other programs. You'll also be able to go through the same step-by-step process to polish your putting game in a companion edition to this book, *Putting In The Zone*, coming in 2019.

NOTES

I WANT TO THANK all the people who have attended our Scoring Zone Schools over the years. This book didn't come together over six months. It was the result of 20 years of collaboration with the enthusiastic students I've been fortunate to work with over those years. I'm also grateful for the hard work from all of my staff. We work as a team, pushing each other to become better teachers and coaches tomorrow than we were today. Ray and Jan Plote invited me to start my golf school at White Deer Run Golf Club all those years ago, and it has been a wonderful relationship. Matt Rudy helped get the thoughts out of my head and onto paper, and Tim Oliver's creative expertise making this book flow and look so good.

TODD SONES owns and operates the Todd Sones Impact Golf Center at White Deer Run Golf Club in Vernon Hills, IL. He has been recognized as both a *Golf Magazine* Top 100 and *Golf Digest* 50 Best Teacher, and is a two-time Illinois PGA Teacher of the Year. *PGA Magazine* named him one of the Top 50 Growth of the Game professionals every year from 2013 to 2016. Sones has worked with Scott McCarron, Joe Durant, Chip Beck, Robert Gamez, Paul Goydos, Steve Jones, Shaun Micheel, Jay Williamson, Stephanie Loudon and Hilary Lunke, among other tour players. This is his third book. For more information, visit **toddsones.com**.

MATTHEW RUDY is *Golf Digest*'s Senior Instruction Writer, and the co-author of more than 30 golf, business and peak performance books with experts like Hank Haney, Dave Stockton, Stan Utley and Dr. Michael Lardon. You can find more about him at **rudywriter.com**.

TIM OLIVER has designed numerous cover stories as *Golf Digest*'s art director, along with books by Phil Mickelson, Tom Watson and Nick Faldo and some of America's top professional golf instructors. He is also the author of the book *Finding Fifteen*. Find him at **timothypoliver.com**.

All photography provided by Hector Padilla

HECTOR PADILLA has been in print production, photography for over 42 years and currently serves as both Graphic and Creative Director for a global retail communications company. **hpadillaprgolf@yahoo.com**.

Made in the USA
Monee, IL
20 June 2020